BLACK DOVES FLY
TO FREEDOM

BLACK DOVES FLY TO FREEDOM

A BOOK OF POEMS
CONCERNING HISTORY,
STRUGGLE, AND PROGRESS

ERICA STEPHENS

NEW DEGREE PRESS
COPYRIGHT © 2021 ERICA STEPHENS
All rights reserved.

BLACK DOVES FLY TO FREEDOM
A Book of Poems Concerning History, Struggle, and Progress

ISBN	978-1-63676-493-1	*Paperback*
	978-1-63730-409-9	*Kindle Ebook*
	978-1-63730-410-5	*Ebook*

This book is dedicated to the ongoing fight for equity, justice, and freedom globally.

Thank you to my amazing family and friends who helped teach me the importance of hard work and leading by example.

CONTENTS

NOTE FROM THE AUTHOR

PART 1.   **OUR BEGINNINGS**

Mother Africa
The Land of Pyramids
Syllables I Speak
A Poem on Early Trade
The Greatness of Africa
African Enslavement
Zanj Rebellion
Africa's Discovery of America
The Ban on White Enslavement
Rainy Mornings in July
Colonization

PART 2.   BLACK ATLANTIC BLUES

A Cry for Help
Death by Me
The Riptides Still Come In
The White Lion
Sugarcane
The Declaration of Dependence
The Body of a Slave
Rosebud Thorns
Music Is
Her Cells
The Black Womb
Natural Beauty
A Taste of Freedom
1865

PART 3.   THE REBIRTH OF AMERICA

Oh, Greenwood
The Greensboro Four
A Poem to Birmingham
Sounds of Silence
The Fisherman's Last Cast
Protest to Equality
Selma to Montgomery
A Man's Tongue
Now, I See
Black Lives Matter, Too
The Mulberry Tree on Mulberry Row
The Rose of Hope

PART 4. STORIES OF THE BLACK EXPERIENCE

SKIN
The Vulnerability of Blackness
How Do You Raise a Black Child in America?
Our Black Love Pt. I
Our Black Love Pt. II
Before the Covers Rise like Waves
The Greatest Pain
February 10, 2018
Virginity
YOU
"That's Just *My* Preference"
Dear Black People of America
You, The Black Dove

A THOUGHT ...
ACKNOWLEDGEMENTS

NOTE FROM THE AUTHOR

"The first step to understanding your position within the world begins with exposure to the history that came before you. To understand the riots and struggles of today, you must examine the riots and struggles of yesterday and the years before. When we know who we are historically, we paint a different picture of ourselves and give hope to the future."

-ERICA STEPHENS

Seven minutes and forty-six seconds is all it took to end a Black man's life in America. One sixteenth of a second is all it took to rewrite a Black woman's future and replace it with R.I.P. Rest in peace to the countless men and women whose faces flashed across my television screen, trended on my Instagram feed, and whose souls relocated themselves to a space outside of this cruel world.

When a man's head is pinned to the ground and blood rushes to his temple, he has no choice but to lay and comfort himself in his own blood. What does death do to a person when they can't seem to escape its presence? It traumatizes them in the most subtle way. A way that appears almost nonexistent until you turn on your television screen and there it is again.

It is with no surprise when I say that the criminal justice system in America was not created to serve justice. In my opinion, it was created for the criminalization, exploitation, and dehumanization of those who were never supposed to be in this "land of the free, home of the brave." I agree when I am presented with the argument that "there are good and bad people in every profession," but there is a reason why America held its breath as Derek Chauvin's verdict was read.

Look at the percentage of Black individuals in prison compared to the general population or the percentage of Black families living in food deserts and tell me that something isn't wrong.

Look at the representation of Black bodies in the media and tell me that something isn't wrong.

The pen and paper I use to write this message have continuously provided me an outlet for self-expression, especially in times where spoken word could not convey my message. Writing, more specifically poetry, allows me to speak directly from my soul with power and emotion. In more recent times, I find poetry essential to my daily routine as a way to deal with traumatic experiences related to violence in America.

The circumstances surrounding the death of George Floyd truly pushed me over the edge and prompted me to write this book. As I stood in St. Louis, Missouri, only miles away from where the death of Michael Brown took place, I couldn't help but question, "How did society get to the point where it is today?" For many Americans, violence inflicted on the Black body has become normalized in ways that are not only unnatural but unacceptable. How did we come to view "Black on Black" crime as a bigger issue than police brutality or normalize the agreed upon narrative that Black America's history began with enslavement?

Educational inequality, for me, is one of the more prominent factors affecting progression on individual and communal levels. As a student growing up, I was rarely exposed to my cultural history, and even then, it was extremely limited. As I worked more within the educational realm, I realized that stories of the Black experience needed to be recorded and shared. I realized that we needed to push back the timeline of Black history and explore events pre-enslavement. In exploring these events, we create a new narrative of "Blackness" in America, highlight the resilience of the Black body, and give hope to the future.

Black Doves Fly to Freedom is a collection of poetry that works to increase our emotional intelligence as it relates to understanding modern day events. I chose poetry to speak directly from the soul and encapsulate the emotions associated with each moment. This book is divided into four sections looking at African history, the Middle Passage, modern day movements, and stories of the Black experience.

The poems presented within this book are based on real events that have occurred. These odes serve as a starting point towards understanding Black history in a deeper context. It is important to note that this is not an exhaustive list of events, and there are many more people, contributions, and intersectional experiences that are not depicted. This book allows us to travel through time and remind ourselves that Black people are beautiful humans!

If you are reading this book, you are a progressive leader passionate about transforming the way in which we think about history. While this book is meant for everyone, poetry lovers, progressive leaders, and those passionate about discussions that drive equity will find this book extremely meaningful. After reading this book, you will feel more educated on topics as they relate to Black history and better understand the link between history and pressing demands of today.

My dream is for everyone who places their hands on this book to read it from cover to cover and reflect. Each line holds meaning and is transformative if you read with intent. My goal is for America and the entire world to see the beauty amongst differing cultural backgrounds. If we value each other, we must make efforts to learn about each other's history. As Nelson Mandela once said, "Sometimes it falls upon a generation to be great. You can be that great generation." By opening this book, you are working to understand modern day circumstances. Thank you for being a leader of generational change.

PART I

OUR BEGINNINGS

Mother Africa

Erupting skies over Giza burst rapidly,
throwing fiery specs of plasma
which spread and disperse heat
for the arrival of the Supreme

Her framework extends
from the ancient pyramids of Egypt
to the mixed quartzite of Cape Agulhas
whose surface holds leaf-like lichen
and yellow dust smelling of orange paint
formless like powder

Her roots cling firmly to soil
and bear root
to all mysteries of the universe

Her root caps submerge,
gulping majestic seas,
opening gold chambers
who outpour alluring minerals
like waterfalls of the Amazon

Sweet elegance whispers from her waters
and washes the devil's blood
from her horn where she hangs
bands of culture,
song and dance,
that churn new dialect out an old womb

The fragile seeds in which she carries
grow fruitfully and abundantly
in and outside of their traditional suit

The Land of Pyramids

Have you ever been to the land of pyramids?

A land where rough granulates of sand
press under your feet as you trek towards the Nile

A land where cool breezes of air whistle their tune
to welcome sun rays as they rise behind
the mighty Pyramids of Ancient Egypt

Our ancient Egyptian ancestors lived
along the high waters of the Nile
where the bank flooded each year in July—
moving black soil downstream

Have you ever been to the land of pyramids?
Where people dress in sheath-like gowns
that gleam under the sun?

Where Gods and Goddesses
are pictured as both,
men and women,
human and half-human,
good spirited and bad

Have you ever been to the land of pyramids
whose layers were built
over three thousand years ago
by Pharohs holding the same DNA as you?
The same beauty,

the same confidence
as the one who reads this message

Have you ever been to the land of pyramids
where red skies seem to expand across the universe
and scarab beetles wobble over sand to reach the Nile
where cool breezes whistle a tune to welcome
our mighty ancestors of Ancient Egypt

Syllables I Speak

The origins of my history
rest between the necks
of Cameroon and Nigeria,
countries whose roots
developed passageways
for my village to expand by foot
and migrate as far as their legs would travel

They traveled East
through tropical rainforests
and listened to the sound
of the augur buzzard shriek

Their movement was waves along the desert,
waves that keep surging higher and higher,
waves whose currents changed with every language spoken

Gbo ti tè mi
Mo lu ilu gan gan mi
Bi mo sé n rin ni ibi giga
Mo n lu ilu gan gan na sare ni kikan
Titi ti owo mi koni isakoso
Mo lu ilu gan gan mi
Bi mo sé n rin ni ibi giga
Mo n lu ilu gan gan na sare ni kikan
Titi ti owo mi koni isakoso

My tongue speaks syllables,
my body catches the rhythm of beats

I press my feet to the ground,
paving routes to unexplored destinations

I press my feet to the ground for
each culture,
each religion,
each opinion
that surrounds me

A Poem on Early Trade

Great dunes of the Sahara
greet me before daybreak

I limp, shifting weight on each leg
under the heat's brutality

My strength mines abrasive sand
that oozes infection out my shell
and radiates an aching pain

I gather my camel, my ship of the land
and set out to reach destinations
that past the heat of the Sahara

I lead as Khabir* in good and stormy light,
sandstorms rise swooping salt over feet,
and venomous creatures stare at my legs
ready to strike with any moment

Wells line themselves from Morocco to Sudan,
watering tired souls on the verge of expiration

Rich African Empires hold 'gold dust'
between quill and trade for new goods
though the main item was grain

Salt led to a fight over power,
overtaking smaller land
with dominance through armies

I follow the wind of West Africa
through the rivers of Niger and Senegal
in search of more income
and a purpose bigger than gold

* Caravan leader

The Greatness of Africa

We rose with greatness from the mud within Earth,
making wild rice to increase our kin

We walked between the Bani and Niger Rivers,
for trade, for wealth, for power, for gold

Without rules to bow down,
we saw the beauty of each other
and guided by the vessel of spirits and strength within

Merchants bowed down to God, as they stood
outside markets whose small colorful baskets
were filled by millet and grain produced by fertile plains

My fingertips spin wet soil,
breaking and pinching it up to form clay vessels,
transforming them into terracotta figures
that depict the various emotions of mankind

Dried shards combine to form a new name: calabash
which hold: the smell of honey, salt of dried fish,
patterns of cloth, cur of milk, and firewood collected
from near the Bani River, twelve miles away, where
waters consumed land long before our footprints,
then lessened back into deep soil

Water splashes as I mold damp clay into ceramic,
holding jewels wished for by Romans, people traveling afar

New buildings rise as I mold,
filling patterns of Sudano-Sahelian
designs of Mali's Great Mosque of Djenné,
whose mud-brick cover
create arched gateways that amaze
and give praise to, the original

Nature's wind blows erosion over great lands with history,
leaving no writing, but sculptures of clay to enjoy
the Greatness of Africa

African Enslavement

Enslavement in Africa was enslavement of men with skill

Men with dignity, respect, and class
that does not place them with the bottom

They were treated as human

Men who relied
on the hands of other men
to churn the waterways
of rich African kingdoms
to produce more wealth,
rather than other Kingdoms of the land

Men not merely just enslaved to their more distant kin

Society's argument to justify enslavement
is that Africans upheld enslavement
but the portion they forget is that
African enslavement was not enslavement as we know it

African enslavement was built on skill not servitude:
think guards, officers, builders building walls
that encompass new ideas and stories
passed down from generation to generation

With White enslavement
skill laborers were targeted
to build the captors nation,

men were forced to use their skill
to produce the narrative
we are ingrained with

Zanj Rebellion

The scar tissue of my skin runs deep,
speaking words before my voice projects

Bruised brown blood erupts from underneath
encasing old pain in new forms
that show a glimpse of a painful moment
but not an entire journey's components

I, along with other Bantu people,
walk angrily amongst Arab salt marshes
who look at me as a wanted source of labor
but unwanted human

I walk with other men who lead
and wait for the signal to rise and rebel

Men and women climbed over top each other
paving their own pathway back home,
we all shout and rage at our captors
we resist work even though
we are subject to beatings and other forms of violence

The whimper of fallen Zanj people can be heard
from within the depths of the salt marsh,
we plead for release from the hands
that make us bleed for their happiness

Rebellion is the only solution
when men won't give us freedom,

when men make us bloody our bodies
in fierce wars

The Zanj Rebellion was for me,
and you, the Bantu people then,
and Bantu descendants now

Africa's Discovery of America

With a thought that there is land
beyond the coast of Mali,
Mansa Musa sends two hundred ships
to discover land beyond what the eye can see

Wild currents extend
that take out 199 ships,
leaving only one boat
to share the story
of the Great Storm

More men navigate
to reach the Americas
and greet inhabitants
with a smile and attempt at genuine connection
instead of a goal to conquer

Yam, sweet potato, cotton, and plantain
crossed seas as evidence of Africans in America

We carved Mandinka script* as evidence
that the Western savior, Christopher Columbus,
was not one of the firsts to discover America:

Ga gya Birds Kpa nde ngbe Ka go ne
Sama(elephant) ga ka bi kpa
Ni ngbe nde kai Sama gya Sun (ga kpa)
Pe kpe gbe nge gya
De kpa ne mbe nde bi-nu gya

Gya pe ndɛgyi ngba kai ga
Gyi nde pɛ du ke nu
Ga gyi Sun

* Known as The Elephant Slabs

The Ban on White Enslavement

Shackles gripped around the ankles of enslaved whites
and hit the same pressure point
as their enslaved African counterparts

Before the sun rose in the East and set in the West,
the European slave did not belong only to others,
they belong to each other

The old version of "White-on-White" crime,
White men kneeled over
and accepted the welts of punishment also

White men owned each other
and diseased the streets of Europe,
causing the city's center to shatter into pieces

Who will work the streets and fields of Europe?

White men and White women
alongside others to grow wealth
except their slavery will end
because the world recognizes
how wrong it is to enslave
because of one man's laziness

Europe placed a ban on slavery,
Now who will work the streets and fields of Europe?

Who holds the power to advance societies,

to clean us from the disease of Europe,
to redirect us and make us wealthy again?

I can grip around the ankles of Africans with shackles
and hit the same pressure points
as I did when enslaving their White counterparts

Rainy Mornings in July

Mother Africa's flesh has been darkened
by the outside world, darkened by
new challenges and diseases discovered
beneath her skin

The roots to her foundation have grown old
but her children, you and I, we play
as she continues to work and defend
against the face of new men: European

What are we to think of our strongest leaders
our fine craftsmen, cooks, artisans, militants
gone, like rain on a Tuesday morning in July

Africa's resources were plentiful,
full of gold, ivory, copper, and pepper,
crops that were tended to daily
until their natural harvest

What nice children we were
to trust new people
and invite them into our world
with a kind heart,
to trust them
even though
they hurt us

Where do we go
when we feel hopeless
on rainy mornings in July?

When men and women are forced to leave Africa,
how can we give hope to children
when a generation of light is missing?

Where do we go
when we feel hopeless
on rainy mornings in July?
and there is only me to fight against the Europeans
as they push past me to enter my homeland
and inflict violence,
brutality,
sickness
and pain on my people?

Colonization

The foundation for my country
has been weakened to a scarlet dust palette,
leaving molecules to fly
along varied patterns in the wind

Africa holds gaps where stone used to stand,
an imperfect country but perfect for colonizers
to swoop in and fix her
steal her natural minerals

The top layer of her soil used to be fertile and bear fruit
but now, she can't seem to bear anything
but sadness and destruction

Her tribes used to speak their languages freely,
share wealth willingly and welcome outsiders
who claimed they traveled to share the Gospel,
colonizers only used the Gospel
to turn our tribes against our tribes

Colonizers snatched native ideals away,
leaving no original language nor religion,
no specific roots for me to trace back to
unless I look at my roots
as the entire continent of Africa

I want to know what tribe my people belonged to

When tribe turned against tribe,
men traveled through the mouth
of the Niger and Congo
and took advantage of rivalry

We used to lead by tribe, in groups
but as soon as colonization came,
things changed to every man for himself

We boarded wet, wooden rooms,
labeled each other as captured vs. uncaptured,
and allowed generations of Africans
to be forced from their homelands

Colonization was planned

It was gradual

It was the reason why Africa slid
like tectonic plates and now
we can't seem to restructure her

Can we revive Mother Africa?

Can we overpower the effects of colonization?

Join as one and label ourselves all as descendants
instead of excluding one another
based on the direction of a boat

PART II

BLACK ATLANTIC BLUES

A Cry for Help

Setting sail off the shores of Nigeria
Ala's* presence commands itself
as violent waves crash
against wood of the Wanderer's bow

Sounds of hesitation overrun
by sounds of hesitation play in my ear,
as a man runs drum solos
down the length of my skin

Another captive screams,
frightening the precious soul
of a newborn onboard,
releasing a fear
unknown by sight
but felt in spirit

Deep welts blemish my dermis
unleashing a deep red,
that flows out of my skin

My blood mixes with the blood of another captive
as she tries to heal me
by applying pressure
with the force of her mouth

Don't stop my bleeding

Take me back home
where oil palm trees sway calmly
against the Atlantic's tempestuous storms,
where Mother Africa calls me in
with the caress of her arms
and tells me that I'm home again,
I won't have to feel lost or confused,
I can allow tears to flow freely from my eyes
because I'm home

* God

Death by Me

Barefoot and bareback,
the salt waters of Savannah, Georgia greet us kindly
before helping plunge our souls back into Heaven

Groups of white heron wail from above
angered by a mix of flesh scraping metal
and droplets of blood becoming one
with the ocean floor

If not death by me, then death by he?

Strawberry shaped grapevines
planted themselves in the distance,
whispering sweet tunes
which become bitter past sundown

As liquid sunshine bows down,
chains link and we stand up,
a reflection of guidance by Chiukwu
who lives within us

If not death by me, then death by he?

Death whirls amongst waves,
limitless, boundless,
without a way to recover
through the seagrass of the sea floor

Bodies, a body,
I am midnight's creature
torn at the brain
slain, strained, maintained by a chain
I am midnight's formless creature

If death by me,
I say:

mmụọ mmiri du anyi bịa, mmụọ mmiri ga-edu anyi laghachi
The water brought us; the water will take us away

The Riptides Still Come In

The pieces you left of me have shattered
over the water's edge and sailed away with you

The riptides still come in as the fish swim out,
pressured against the water's current:
a grace perfected by death

With my lack of final goodbye,
I am weakened

My chance is gone
to share words
I wish I had shared,
and now, I am haunted
by everything I kept inside

How would I have known that you
would be taken away from me?

You left me without choice,
but if you loved me,
you would have fought to stay,
to live out our dreams
even if faced with death

Do I matter to you now?

Here in Badagry, Nigeria,
the riptides still come in

Mentally they pull me and I push,
struggling to breathe
because you
are no where
to be found

Will I ever see you again?

My last memory with you
is all I am left to replay,
us running along the coast,
waves crashing
as the sun and sky met
and we confessed our love to each other

Men came
and tore you
away from me,
my greatest moment
turned
into my worst nightmare

I miss the shape
of your cheekbones
pressed against mine,
the brown of your eyes
illuminated by the day's sun,
the hard callus on your palm
after a day's work

Will I ever see you again?

Then, we can share new secrets,
radiate the sounds of our voices
like echoes off underwater caves
that only we will understand

The pain I feel away from you
wears like an open sleeve,
skin exposed from a fresh wound,
a scar that I am forced to be reminded of daily

The riptides still come in,
but they don't let me reach you

If I find you one day,
will you recognize me
from the softness of my skin
or the texture of my hair?

Watching the riptide, I pray for you and ask:

Will I ever see you again?

The White Lion

I was pushed down
the stairs of The White Lion
by men firmly holding loaded guns

Faces I used to see in my village
appeared to me in thin air
and I reached for the sky
trying to grab onto them
for a quick escape

O que você está procurando?

From the ship's deck,
I heard the sound of children cry,
I heard the splash of people
being thrown over the boat's edge,
by force and by choice

I saw bleeding flesh when I closed my eyes
and smelled dead flesh when I inhaled,
so I tried to look at the world around me
and focus on what was soon to come

¡No mires de esta manera!

The White Lion made me find happiness
between the thin space
separating my sanity and inner thoughts

Unknowing of where life's next step would take me,
I saw the sea as a way for me
to travel back to the Kingdom of Kongo
and tell others
how the Portuguese captured me in the dead of dark

Soyez silencieux!

If I was African in Africa,
can I still be African wherever you take me?

Can I still speak Kikongo?

Can I say to myself,
Nzambi kele ve na kati ya bantu

Take me back
to the same location
The White Lion
picked me up at
and let Africa be home

Sugarcane

The small hard seed
of a sugarcane plant
is nonexistent
when hidden,
wrapped inside
the darkness of my fist
then thrown away

When the sugarcane tree reaches light
and all its dreams of life
are ready to unfold,
its roots stretch
beyond the wetness
felt beneath our feet
as they soak
into the topics mush

The sweetness of cane
can be smelled over distances,
and wrapped around the lips
for a slow suck of sugar

With bold flavor,
it makes the mouth
squirt juices back
into the greenish blue
seas it grew from

When I chop sugarcane,
I chop it by the root
and watch its head
bobble ^{up} and _{down},
like free men
in their own world

The taste of sugar grows
in hot mills where
a feeder cuts cane into small pieces
with the sharpness of a machete,
extracting juices that boil til thick

Temperatures make me faint,
liquid heat makes me burn,
but I strain liquid cane
and dry it til the sugar crystals
fall down over top of me

Sugarcane makes boats blow
over the coast
from Jamaica,
to Dominica, to Haiti
in search of Obeah men
who can heal me
from becoming lost in my worries
as I chop brown roots of sugarcane

The Declaration of Dependence

We hold onto lies to uphold confusion,
we whitewash history the same way
our founding fathers did
because modern-day fruit
doesn't fall too far
from the old tree
it was created by

How much more could we want
when we have life, liberty,
and the pursuit of happiness?

Our freedoms have been replaced
with disrupted and destructed forms of government
that ignore the core of important issues
and blame each and every one of us
for who we are and our situations

You crave when it clicks
that the Declaration of Independence
is really a Declaration of Dependence

An outdated document
created for government
and the idea that
history will be sure
to repeat itself over
and over and over, again

The Body of a Slave

My body is a gruesome reflection
of the slave trade,
tattered clothing
with tattered thoughts,
happiness overrun by
horrific scenes play
in my mind
on repeat

Raised welts crisscross, *tic-tac-toe*
stinging as I heal myself
with an application of alcohol

Men don't like to be alone
when it's cold outside,
when life is fearless,
whipping you without remorse

Let me die beside her or beside him,
let me caress the grave marker of my mother
and feel her love one more time

My black body is strong
but it's not invincible

Rosebud Thorns

running

Rosebud thorns speak to me
as they dig into the soles of my feet,
and tears speed toward my ears

My spirit guide protects me
from evil praying to enter
and reduce my health to sickness

Where are my people?

Somewhere amongst the rosebuds' thorns
I found the Underground Railroad,
dried footprints beside a wall of blossoming roses

Rosebud thorns speak to me
as they dig into the soles of my feet,
and say, "Keep going"

Music Is

I clap my hands twice
to create a beat that
fills the wind of the Earth

It sends sound waves traveling,
from my ear throughout my body

My mind and heart synchronize
to produce a steady beat,
my eyes close and I tilt my head
towards the sky

A low hum begins to flow outside of me,
and I begin to sing an interlude softly

It fades

Hums soothe my heart
forcing me to pause
and focus on
the power of healing
that derives when music
escapes from within
to bring joy from sorrow

The music I hum
is my time capsule,
my release from the wicked screams
that bounce around my brain
as frightful memories

Drums are my protection,
instruments that lift my spirit,
as their speed
becomes faster and faster
and my soul releases
like blue flames from hot fires

Music is my medicine

I listen to music
because its words
invite me
to share my inner rage

Music is my medicine,
my capsule to travel outside
the confines of plantation farmland
that wraps me up and spits me out on repeat

Music is my mental release
in high and low pitches,
a way to expose myself
to love and healing
and return back to a time
where music wasn't just my therapy,
it was my happiness

Her Cells

Henrietta?

Darling,

where
are
you?

My nostrils
take in
your smell,
the drip of
fresh blood,
cells shedding
from the lining
of your cervix,
staining
porcelain
white tubs
scented with
eucalyptus,
tea tree oil,
and twelve petals
that follow
small ripples

Your HeLa cell
birthed America
for the immortal

soul she is today,
a sample
of your bloody cells
grown on a clear
petri dish,
taken without
your permission
for the growth
of medicine

Why do we
still not know
your name,
even when
you live
in all of us?

Henrietta,
A Black woman
with roots from Clover, Virginia
saved humanity with
sharp uterus pain
that made her cry out
and caress her cervix
in a bathtub
scented with
eucalyptus,
tea tree oil,
and twelve petals
that follow
the trail
of her blood

A Black woman
saved humanity
even when
she didn't
give permission;
Who will save
the Black women
who drip
fresh red blood
in porcelain
white bathtubs
as they scream
in pain
without relief

The Black Womb

Ram two inches
of a cold speculum
inside my vagina
and watch me squirm
like worms in a can
as you increase the width
of your instrument
to examine my insides

The iron under my head
is my only comfort
in old gynecology rooms
where my chained legs
remain pinned
by metal guards
so cold
they burn patches
in my skin

From the end of my ankle
to the high of my thigh,
my legs are cages
opening a rare land
where diamond jewels reside,
where doves fly
squawking melodies
in high pitch,
and pink sweet peas
dance their fragrance

within the wind

Where is my medicine?

When I lay down
to forceful pushes
on my cervix,
I feel pain

I feel the pain of
Anarcha, Betsey, and Lucy
as they bled,
on hard tables,
cup after cup,
for you to know
gynecology

Gynecology came by
Black women's bodies,
our wombs dismantled
without remorse,
tears pooled in our pupils
and streamed from our eyes,
slid down both cheeks,
until they appeared on metal tables
and eventually hit the floor like rain,
drop by drop
until there were none left

Gynecology came by
Black women's pain,
but Black women

still can't feel pain
because doctors attack them
with statements like
"She's fine" and "She's overreacting,"
ridiculing them
and leaving them to sit for hours
in cold waiting room
until their wombs turn red
and all they feel
is blood escaping

The Black womb is Gynecology
so why is the Black womb
not appreciated?

Natural Beauty

How beautiful am I
when I am at rest?

Thin skin drooped over the retina of my eye,
you watch me from afar
memorized by the idea
that a woman could have
such a high degree
of natural beauty

I can be your Beauty
and your Beast,
a Black beast,
with locs that grow
against the law of gravity,
twisting,
turning,
interlocking
with each strand

The grip of my hand
is my creation,
a way to part hair
then spread oil
evenly like butter

My beauty is seasoned
like cinnamon and sugar
in chai lattes:

Add a little more spice in summer,
a little less during winter,
lighten and darker with each season

Naturally, my curls form
from the root of my head,
patterns ranging from 3A to 4C
I am a Black Queen with curls

Where did natural beauty go
before it was exchanged
for lighter skin tones,
perms that turned hair bone straight,
BBLs in the shape
of plastic promises of confidence,
and the false idea that natural beauty
is somehow less worthy?

I used to conform to the norm of America
before realizing that my natural beauty
is the norm that America wants to follow

How beautiful am I
when I am at rest?

Thin skin drooped over
the retina of my eye,
you watch me from afar
memorized by the idea
that a woman could have
such a high degree
of natural beauty

A Taste of Freedom

The black pigmentation stored
within the genome of my skin
holds the bruises of freedom
turned over twice then beaten
inside a granite mortar with
three pestles until granular specs
of fine powder circulate like dust

Dark purple is the new paint of my flesh;
A color so dense, it appears black
under a midnight sky,
tracing my path,
an unexplored constellation

The blackness of my berry is the sweetness of my roots
densely packed into a body so powerful
it crossed three seas,
two deserts,
and one continent
against her will
but still survived

Dark, sulky blood clots my veins
after a good Sunday's work,
swelling my innermost organs,
filling them instead with blood of the U.S.A.

Earth's sun holds no mercy
as it turns on its axis each day,
giving light to twelve hours of labor
followed by ten hours of striking

When will it end it?
My struggle to build a world where I am not accepted,
a world that dresses my soul in pain,
twirls me around for self-excitement,
and spits me out like black dip in country fields

I am the taste of freedom for myself,
a taste so delectable it burns,
sending those who envy
back to the ashes they rose from

Around my frame,
my blackness is sacrifice
shipped off the coast of Africa
then gifted a taste of freedom by Abraham

What is struggle
wrapped around the brain
then pulled tight without progress?

What are Black women and Black men
without each other,
when their hands are blistered,
and throats are punctured
from the prick of a thorn in Spring?

The future of America
is the pen of Abraham
pressed down firmly
with a quill dozed in ink
tracing over paper made from hemp

The Black body seems expendable
until we examine its bruises deeply
to find a struggle and fight so intense
that it produces for itself

A Taste of Freedom

1865

For the past twenty-six years,
I looked down to rusty shackles
tight around my wrists

Bruises turned them purple,
until one day they
up and fell off

I was told through the grapevine
that I'm a man free now

Free to roam
the plains of the South
until I reach the North

Then, there
I will make sure
that torture
will never reach me again

PART III

THE REBIRTH OF AMERICA

Oh, Greenwood

The dirt roads of Tulsa
don't ride the same
since blood from the Tulsa Riots
sunk into the bedrock of the city
and became the root
for which all fruit bears

I remember watching blood spray from a man I once knew
like water spurting from the mouth of a garden hose,
covering cracks and crescents engraved
into imperfect sidewalks and side-buildings

Black Wall Street lived in Greenwood,
an area where black business supported black business,
uplifted it,
watched it grow,
and invested
over and over again,
an area where the happiness of Black families
could be felt by their natural smiles
and the sight of couples walking their children to school,
an area where White men would come
just to stare into the faces of peaceful Black men,
angered only by their skin color and associated success

It was an allegation of Dick Rowland raping Sarah Page
in the Drexel Building that sparked gunfire in Tulsa

Green grenades were implanted in nurseries
and bombs painted red music notes
on the remains of city streets
where thriving business once stood

The bloody exchanges of Greenwood taught me
that even if a Black man is alleged to have done something,
him and his community will always reap the consequences

Oh, Greenwood

I remember the magnolias that grew from your root,
red like the bedrock it grew from,
strong like the descendants who once lived here,
delicate like the history created by Tulsa's bloody massacre

The Greensboro Four

"Boy, get up!
 I said get up!
Gon' now,
 I said get up!"

Or what Sir?

Ever since I came to Greensboro, NC
life has been nothing but Hell

I walk, I'm harassed
I eat, I'm harassed
I protest peacefully, I'm harassed,
so what more do you want from me?

I twist around on my barstool seat
to find us, four silent Black men
at a slick, glossy empty counter

"Leave!" the White waitress screams
as she walks past me to take a White
man two sunny-side up eggs

Lady, I ain't leaving

"I ain't gonna to tell you again"

I'm not leaving so get ready to repeat yourself

A policeman walks in with his baton,
"All colored folk who ain't supposed to be in here.
Get out!"

I'm not leaving

The policeman paces back and forth,
strikes the chair next to me
and looks directly into my eyes

My underarms begin to sweat,
so I remind myself of the reason
I sit-in: for respect

He kicks my chair with his feet,
producing a vibration so hard
I feel it throughout my body and jolt

He laughs. "You just a boy, ain't you?"

No, I'm a man that knows his rights,
knows his freedom, and his worth

He pounds the baton hard to the ground

I am numb

"You know the rules!"

I sure do Sir

I refuse to be disrespected

I refuse to allow segregation
I refuse to allow—

 policeman spits on me

I refuse to allow you
to distract me from my mission

I continue to sit and listen
to a single jazz record play
underneath an uproar of people
angry about a peaceful movement,
a sit-in for justice

A Poem to Birmingham

I first heard about you
on the front cover
of a history book
in sixth grade

History, where
old trauma and new mindsets collide,
where written notes are shared
for girls like me
to learn about girls
like Addie Mae Collins,
Cynthia Wesley,
Carole Robertson,
and Carol Denise McNair
whose eyes remind me of mine

I turn page after
page after page
until I see a shattered
16th Street Baptist Church

Birmingham, how could you allow this?

I know you saw little girls
being dressed
by their mothers
and walked to Sunday School

Freshly cleaned bathtubs
filled with bubble bath,
white dresses turned inside out for ironing,
black tights ripped then replaced,
ballet flats slipped on slowly
just as new curls were released
and stretched down the length of backs

Red kisses placed to their foreheads
as they rushed out the door,
eager to meet other little Black girls
whose dresses twirled as they strolled down 16th Street

"Mama, what is the Pastor going to preach today?"

"I don't know, baby.
We'll have to wait and see what the Lord brings to
His heart."

"Mama, do you believe in angels?"

"I do. Baby, I believe in everything God does:
His miracles, His blessings, His hurt,
even when I can't seem to understand."

"Mama, do you love me?"

"I sure do love you. Love you with all the breath I have."

And if four mothers knew
that would be the last way
they told their daughters goodbye,

would they still dress them up
in white from head to toe?
Lay a single string of pearls
around their neck and
walk them to Sunday School?
Slip a pair of fresh ballet flats on slowly,
just for at least ten sticks of dynamite
to infringe the insides of their precious little girls
until they explode

Daughters who wanted nothing more
than to stare at stained, multicolored panes
and listen to the Preacher at
16th Street Baptist Church

Birmingham,
how could you allow
Addie Mae Collins,
Cynthia Wesley,
Carole Robertson,
and Carol Denise McNair
to become angels before their time?

Sounds of Silence

Listen

                        To the prevailing westerlies
              that blow east-west across the North,
stretching thirty to sixty degrees in latitude-
                    wind consistent in whistle
                and commanding my presence

                    From 6 a.m. to 10 p.m.
        sun shines down from clear, blue skies
      and the westerlies play warm jazz tunes,
         producing sounds like those from
       gold brass mouthpieces of saxophones,
           players deliver tunes so gentle
         they enter my soul and allow me to
            indulge in the world's beauty

                When the clock strikes 10 p.m.
the small yellow crescent of the moon rises high,
  waxing frightening silhouettes in the darkness

Air sweeps through the tattered branches of oak trees,
        whose green, lobed leaves and brown nuts
                have been replaced
    with the distinct tilted heads of Black bodies
who remain tightly secured to branches by twisted brown
                                  rope

Silence is a message.

A deprivation of the voice,
a hard hand over my mouth and yours,
a chokehold on words,
a stifle of the inner voice that fills my mind,
navigating me even when I fail to act

When the westerlies flow through
pockets of my exposed hanging skin,
Who will listen to my message?

Silence is a man's greatest power
and his greatest weakness

Trust

That Malcolm X and MLK Jr.
were not greengrocers without reason,
men scavenging the fields of open minds,
feeding on the seed of education
to project words that guide, lead, and push
new generations to freedom

The tree under which we bear fruit
has fallen and tumbled into the sea,
waves stronger than the privilege that defines America

Who am I?

An American with no privilege by race,
privilege in opportunity that is gifted
at the expense of lost stolen identity

The Black man did not begin with Mr. X
nor did it end, but it progressed
like museums of culture:
texts filled by hands
that fold life into crinkles of paper
that sculpt into elegant origami

Black and blue pens are the instruments
for artists once deemed mentally unfit
to share stories that reside within their creative realms

Honored,
I should be,
but in life

Not in death when I am buried,
covered by rich chunks of soil,
knocking from the inside of a locked casket,
waiting for someone to release my soul
back to Earth to hear my tribute of life

With life comes death, but honor my body,
not the silence that comes with my death

Death is silence.

Silence

Was the body of Malcolm X fearless
as he gushed blood over oak floorboards,
turning him back to black ash,
a sacrifice of loyalty to his movement

Silence is separation between life and death,
created by the pull of one trigger
and the release of sixteen bullets
into my cranium and throughout my body;
The westerlies continue to play their song
filling the air with a whistle so clear
that the tilted heads of Black bodies
pleading for mercy
have no reason but to twirl

Silence is death.

The Fisherman's Last Cast

The fury of gray waters
opens life underneath
the slosh of sea floorboards;
Cracked bones and brittle remains
of enslaved Caribbean people
toss themselves upward
whirling fistfuls of ash
toward seashores
filled by the sharp stamp of peach-colored shells
that decorate lifeless bone like pretty caskets

Their shipment destination: UNKNOWN

Fishermen travel on wooden speedboats
carved with machetes by hand
then painted red,
striped yellow,
and circled green
to attract the brittle remains of ancestors
floating underwater in seaweed gardens
whose leaves wave to boats
passing up above

Fluorescent shirts worn by the fishermen
hold in the smell of good oxtail
balanced by rice and peas,
picked fresh by the calloused hands of mothers
who harvest sugarcane

Grey waters pour out notes of reggae
for the year's first carnival,
where orange feathers fall
d
o
w
n

Within the waters
I dance on the tip of my toes to each note,
gracefully swaying until,
day and night collide
and fisherman dressed
in fluorescent shirts
PULL
their last cast

My ancestor's dance
with their cracked bones and brittle remains
under the Caribbean waters,
feasting on peels of plantain
that flow freely through currents,
creating a passageway
back to the mainland

Protest to Equality

My grandmother was born partially free
near the mountaintops of Charleston, West Virginia
where she, a "colored" woman,
used the "colored" restroom
after giving her life away to tobacco fields
owned by White farmers who cared less
if she lived or died in their presence

Her honey-colored skin was discriminated against,
her rights and opportunities diminished
because her outer and inner beauty
was far too mesmerizing for anyone to ignore

She held the pressure of raising my mother and
motivating herself to the highest standard
while being a Black woman in the United States

I call her my grandmother
and she raised her kids well
despite the odds or
hard labor it took
just so I could have a future

My grandmother was born partially free
in a time where protest was her only voice

Without a sign, she seemly had
no interest in the future,
no hope for justice,
no dreams of equality like MLK

MLK had a dream of equal rights
and equal rights came on February 10, 1964,
the same year my mother was born

Where would I be without the Civil Rights Act of 1964?
Where would any of us be,
given that the Civil Rights Act of 1964
created the passageway to equality for all, not just one race

I was born in Virginia as a free woman

Without my grandmother's protest and the protest of others,
being born equal wouldn't be possible

Where would I be without the Civil Rights Act of 1964?

I would be protesting the streets with modern-day MLK,
screaming that I dream for equal rights
because even if
I am labeled as a "colored" women
I am far more than what the eye can see

Selma to Montgomery

Jimmie Lee Jackson was shot and killed on February 26, 1965 in a peaceful march on voting rights. His death helped spark the march from Selma to Montgomery which helped in the passage of the Voting Rights Act of 1965. The officer who shot and killed Mr. Jackson pleaded guilty to manslaughter and served six months in prison.

I heard that Jimmie was a good man,
I missed his funeral
but from the way
his family and friends
elevated his name,
I could just tell
that he was a good man,
and a deacon too

I didn't know him personally,
but I paid my respects
the best way I knew how,
through peaceful protest
even though
that was the same way
'ole Jimmie left us

Freedom is the topic
on everyone's mind these days

Freedom this, freedom that,
but we forget that
freedom is a struggle
that doesn't come
from sitting in silence

Another brother, John Lewis,
led the march from Selma to Montgomery
to further voting rights as a human right
for those of all backgrounds

As I walked,
I heard voices shout phrases like "Voting Rights Now!"
and "If not today, then when."

When we reached Edmund Pettus Bridge,
I didn't expect freedom to be handed to me
nor did I expect
a policeman to strike my body for no reason

I started to run
like the hundreds of other people
protesting alongside me

Alabama state troopers
dressed in black
chased me on their horses

A bloodied stick hit my back hard
as I ran stumbling
through a thick-smoke like substance

I saw an older woman fall,
tried picking her up, but
she was out of my reach

Lord, rest her soul

A trooper grabbed the back of my shirt,
beat me, maced me, beat me
and maced me
until I fell unconscious

This is the price you pay for freedom

When I woke,
news crew cameras flashed in my face,
anchors asked questions
that I couldn't comprehend in the moment,
protesters carried other protesters
by the arms and feet
looking for any way possible
to escape Bloody Sunday's defeat

When the sun rose again,
I stepped back out
side-by-side with nearly 20,000 protestors
and walked over the Edmund Pettus Bridge
in pain but proud

A Man's Tongue

The firmness of a man's wet tongue,
before he speaks,
is a reflection of his own self-trust;
His abstract thoughts run barefoot
from the brainstem to the spinal cord,
illuminating his brain during REM sleep,
running circuits
from the brain to the thalamus,
back to the cortex,
a repeat playlist of fantasies
wild enough to make oneself afraid

Day in and night out,
a man uses his strength:
his tongue,
to taste flavors of deception:
sweet, sour, bitter, salty

Throw your head back and taste

A man's tongue is the unit by which
the world's most powerful
four-letter words flow: love, heal, grow, hope,
free-falling,
like copper pennies thrown
off white mountaintops

A man is his word;
For he is what he says he is,
he is what he shows you,
basking himself
in his own lies,
his own truth

When the temperature of his blood rises
and clear raindrops fall down,
who is a man
when all he has left
is the words
that plummet down
from his tongue

Words projected are contagious,
like yawns in office rooms at 8 am,
setting new standards for wild visions
that capture minds in REM sleep,
violent enough
to make any man
scared of himself,
more than the world
that chases after him
as he speaks for justice

His words are light kisses,
grazed by a filter,
strained like coffee beans
before they turn to cold brew-
because his words are his dreams
and his dreams are too big

for the world to take in,
he'd rather hold his tongue
than strike America with discomfort
with thoughts of equitable progression

A man's tongue
is the source of his energy,
the source of his own truth,
firm and with strength,
words hold power:
one can lead
by the words of a man,
or create a meaning
that has been,
washed ....
words that have been
nuzzled to the core
to taste
the flavors of deception

Now, I See

A string of rubies,
like death of Black men,
is only precious
when broken
in limited supply

Blood drips in my hand
and extends across
the width of my tips-
this man's,
this woman's,
this child's
body,
though lifeless
belongs to me

Horrific screams still fill my ears
because
I am haunted,
traumatized by death
that has been marketed,
bodies,
that have been profited off,
then thrown away,
left only to harden
in black body bags
and caressed
by me

To die Black
in America,
is to fly away
from pain,
tightened
around the neck,
increasing at a pressure
so high that
a scream of
"I can't breathe"
is merely a whisper

Out and in,
I repeat
the mouthing of final words,
hot air released
through
lips that press
against white teeth

Now, I see-

A mother's hurt
is a modern-day trend

To obtain the Black dollar,
America will claim that
Black lives matter,
without pushing
for systems and programs
that make the country more equitable

If human lives are important,
then ending the fear of Blackness
belongs to America

Issues of hard bullets traveling
nine hundred miles per hour,
as they hit bodies,
uncaring of location
is America's

How can America allow for us
to take our last gasp
on car hoods,
in parking lots,
on city streets,
and expect us
not to become upset?

We attempt to fight for justice
even as we take our last breath
despite knowing our personal battle
has already been won

What should we do
before the lights flash,
and we are lifeless,
alone in the darkness,
wishing,
someone, anyone
cared

Xzavier Hill, Linwood Lambert, Henry Dumas, Randolph Evan, George Floyd, Elijah McClain, Philando Castile, Michael Brown, Eric Garner, Alton Sterling, Freddie Gray, Botham Jean, Laquan McDonald, Manuel Ellis, Steven Jerrell Jr., Ahmed Aubrey, Riah Milton, Dominique Fells, Mya Hall, Miriam Carey, Eleanor Bumpurs, Danette Daniels, Kayla Moore, Sheneque Proctor, Aiyana Stanley-Jones, Rita Lloyd, Sandra Bland, Denise Stewart, Alesia Thomas, Breonna Taylor, Akai Gurley, Keith Lamont Scott, Christian Taylor, Tamir Rice, Tony McDade, Evon Young

Black Lives Matter, Too

Is it Black over Blue or Blue over Black?

Human rights or human suits?

Are black hats labeled
with white writing: "Police"
a green light
for beating my flesh
as I plead for mercy?

Black lives matter because human rights matter

Black Lives Matter is not a terrorist group;
It is an organization, a pilot for change
a vessel of hope for a new generation
working towards equity

The world questions, "Do Black lives matter?"
but fail to remember that Black lives
create the world's greatest trends,
hold the world's greatest features,
and persist to greatness

We scream "Black lives matter"
on streets, shouting so that
someone, anyone
will listen

Can Black people be treated as humans like we ask?

Can we walk the street without painting it red?

Can we raise our children before we see them die?

Can we jog in neighborhoods without fearing for our lives?

Right now, it seems the answer is no,
but I ask again: Do Black lives matter?

Everyone loves to mimic Blackness
until it's time to advocate for Blackness

People want to be influenced by Black culture,
to be a part of the culture,
to run the culture
until shots are aimed into our backs,
Now, where are you all who love Black culture?

If you appreciate
the ideals and culture
based on Black people,
please remember that
Black lives matter, too

The Mulberry Tree on Mulberry Row

Twenty-four hours
after a crow sang
under the hot humid heat of July
streams of golden nectar oozed
from orange-brown bark
surrounding the Charlottesville Rotunda

Bluebirds rested quietly
on the curlicues of dark branches
marked by the beauty of those
who chose to chisel
her imperfections away

Darkness fell,
and a sole torch
within the distance
lit the sky

Soon,
one light combined with two lights,
three lights combined with four until
the brightness coming towards me,
was anything but memorizing,
and I said to myself:

Please just let me live,
let me visit
the Mulberry Tree
on Mulberry Row

to meet my ancestors
that created my University,
that created our University
that wore the welts
of punishment,
of depression,
of pain,
just so Thomas Jefferson
could be seen as an idol
in the eye of America

Tiki-torches hold no hate,
but the people who hold them
hold a grudge so intense
that they use light as a scare tactic

Light: a symbol of hope,
a symbol of progression,
a symbol held by the Statue of Liberty,
her torch is a welcome to all
in search of freedom

Isn't this America?

The land of the free,
the home of the brave,
the place where justice and love
should be extended to all,
but instead, we extend hate
as a way to ignore debate,
as a way to further injustice

even when we know
that it's wrong

Darkness fell on August 11, 2017,
and I ran up the mountainside of Monticello
in search of peace

I ran so fast that I fell,
but when I got back up
all I could see was the
beauty of the Mulberry Tree

Mulberry Row at Monticello
is where the beauty of Blackness
transcends from gnarled roots

It's where nectar becomes adhesive
becomes eccentric,
becomes unified like people
hand-in-hand
on Fourth Street
as we honor Heather Heyer
for the beautiful soul she was
and all that she would come to be

Under the Mulberry tree,
love replaces hate,
hate has no place,
those of you
who wish to join us
are free to do so

The Rose of Hope

Hope found itself within the crystal blue waters of
Honolulu
and traced itself back to the mainland of America
where she weathered the bedrock for citizens,
natural born and immigrant, to rise

In the land of America, a dream is not only a dream but,
it is a message of manifestation from within,
pushing for the betterment of one's kind,
despite darkness, trials, and tribulations,
from one's past, present, and future

It is the captured vision of success
eaten halfway off silver plates of white-collar workers
I serve in the evenings,
that push me to go beyond what I might currently be,
for something,
for someone,
greater

and so I reach

stretching further than
the second-class citizen goals society set for me
focusing keenly on the prize like bald eagles
locking in on their prey,
a persistence praised yet envied from afar

Who is America at his worst?

Who is America at his best?

We are persistent, dependable
mustard seeds found within
the lifeless, dank straw of a haystack:
persistent we conquer,
to mold new foundations,
to conquer greatness and set new standards,
to thrive for generations,
to represent diverse populations,
who will reach beyond those generations we see today.
We are the people,
but hope is only found where the people roam together

Where is the hope that lay upon the
surface of crystal blue waters,
surrounded by blue jade vine
and the smell of nectar
off the bank of the Promised Land?

How did our rose of hope stem,
when she grew up from concrete
dreaming to be as blessed as you,
as blessed as me,
as blessed as we,
in America

PART IV

STORIES OF THE BLACK EXPERIENCE

SKIN

The covering of my skin
was never by choice,
but I caress myself
each day
as if it were
the first time
my brown eyes
saw chocolate

Spring's first rain
brings cool droplets
that rush into my pores
and infuse with scents
of whipped shea butter
and succulent honey

I bask myself
under the warmness
of summer's sun
as it darkens me,
minute by minute

My skin is my muse,
a gallery of art
defined by fine lines
and years under the sun's shine,
distinguishing me
and my beauty

The Vulnerability of Blackness

"A local man was killed early Thursday morning after an encounter with police near Maplewood Lane. Witnesses say that children were at the scene of the incident. This is Kelly Johnston, WDBJ 13."

Another man named James
was gunned down by police
while walking his two kids
home from school

Before the shots,
one kid cheerfully yelled "Daddy" on his left arm,
the other cheerfully yelled "Daddy" on his right,

It's small moments like these
that make parenthood exciting for me,
a man who dreams of being a father,
to have kids that sway
from either side of my arm
as I smile to tell them: "I love you."

James reminds me of myself:
tall and slender with dreadlocks that hang low,
a Black man boasting a rich skin tone
and gold chain dangling around his neck

When I said I wanted representation in the media,
I wasn't talking about murder

When I close my eyes, I see him.
I see a man like myself,
minding his business,
only to be wrongly categorized
and shot in 5.2 seconds

It's easy for a father to say "I love you" while living,
but how do you say "I love you" when
you were never able to say "goodbye?"

Who is strong enough to tell children that "Daddy will
never see you again?"

And when they ask "Why?" you must say,
"Because Daddy was Black,
and America doesn't like Black people at times"

Blackness is vulnerability,
and the vulnerability of Blackness
began in the minds of people
who chose to strip Black and Brown bodies
of everything they knew as normal,
people who created a society on
the dehumanization of the Black body
year after year after year
until years turned into decades
and decades turned into centuries

Vulnerability is
me tying a silky, green durag
or fluorescent orange scarf

around my temples
and being labeled as a thug

Vulnerability is
Black women wearing dresses,
being sexually assaulted,
and being told "they deserved it"
because of sick men
who are attracted to
the natural curve of their hip

Vulnerability is
Black men and women
being gunned down
while running, eating, driving,
walking children home from school
on either side of their arm
and losing their life in 5.2 seconds.

Vulnerability is:
1. Not wearing hoodies
2. Not walking behind someone at night
3. Not asking for help
for fear that someone else may feel uncomfortable

Vulnerability is
dreadlocks being seen as a threat
when they are a symbol of pride and culture

Vulnerability is
not knowing

if you will live by sunrise
or die by sunset

Vulnerability is
the pressure to perform,
to conform,
to dissemble your way of life,
to code-switch
from situation to situation
so that you can appear
more "professional"
in the eyes of another

Vulnerability is Blackness,
and Blackness is Vulnerability

How Do You Raise a Black Child in America?

A child whose skin absorbs
bold rays from the sun,
and reflects back bronze
to mother nature

A child whose skin
speaks before skill,
to receive opinions
before their mouth
has ever opened

A child whose complexion
raises questions
as others attempt to determine
what he or she
is mixed with,
when in reality,
their genetic recipe
is Black mixed with Black

Judgements cover the faces
of little Black children
like single masks at Met Galas
though these lay bejeweled
with false assumption

How do you raise a child
whose innocence
is only apparent

ten seconds after birth,
then they are tagged
as free target practice
for violence to shoot its pain
and linger

Police brutality and profiling
are top reasons why
mothers and fathers
give "play-by-plays,"
rules to follow
to maintain one's humanity when:
running,
sleeping,
breathing,
living while Black

Rule #1. Don't be the angry Black woman.
Rule #2. Be careful how you wear your hair to an interview.
Rule #3. Don't walk too close to someone at night.
Rule #4. Keep your hands out of your pockets.
Rule #5. Don't run because

we know the aftermath of running-
two silver bullets
loaded in hard metal,
trigger cocked back then released,
bullets soar into you
like fireworks falling from the sky,
calling you down to your knees

How do you raise a Black child in America?
when their cheerful spirit
is broken each day
by sharp words that carve
insecurity beneath confidence;
A child blamed
for feeling pain,
blind to their own beauty,
clueless like green June bugs tied to string

How do you raise a Black child in America?

A child born without a manual
to view the life they will endure;
A child whose most captivating trait
will be their label as "second class"
even when their intelligence
and good character
set the standard

Why is it normalized
that Black children are
guilty until proven innocent?

A child just wants to be a child.

You raise a Black child
with the strength
of the world
inside your palm,
and carefully place love
at their core

You raise a Black child
with positive affirmations
that hail from the heart,
words so powerful
they have no choice
but to believe
that they are beautiful

You raise a Black child
with the gift of empathy
even if the world
has none for them

You raise a Black child
with the understanding that
their pain is your pain,
their hurt is your hurt,
their smile is your happiness
and their physical body
is your blessing

You raise a Black child
like any other child but,
each day you silently worry
if danger will come,
and if so,
Will you see them again?

Our Black Love Pt. I

The slow stroke of his fingertips
on my skin
reminds me
what it means
to be a real woman;
A real Black woman
with hips that drip melanin
and become full,
attempting to overtake his body,
and sprinkle pleasure
like pixie dust

Pressed,
body-to-body,
my full lips touch and repel
casting addictive spells of love
which remain hidden
under layers of gloss
filled by the smell
of petroleum jelly
and mint

At the crossroads of his thoughts,
I am his best friend, lover, and temptation
His bad girl,
His reason for releasing
rivulets that slide s l o w l y
from the corners of his eyes,
as I stroke "S"

outward, inward, outward,
on the right side
of my rosy canvas

Waves of silence
flow overtop us
and we stare,
brown eyes
gazing into
brown eyes,
mesmerized
by the sight
of each other

The love that climaxes
from the innermost portion
of my soul is for him.
It is consistent,
understanding
of all thoughts
that worry him

Are you okay, my love?
The shape we carry dies
like the bodies we age in,
but my love for him
is permanent

My love is his love
without regret,
fine material cut
from the same cloth,

locked with beauty
on the Pont des Arts
for the world to admire

His caress
is as delicate,
as slow strokes
of his fingertips
used to paint
new images
of Our Black Love

Our Black Love Pt. II

The beauty of her eyes capture me,
even more than the curve of her hips
multiplied by the taste of her lips

Light touches
from her fingertips
to my frame
send shock waves
as she presses
her palm
to my soul,
reaching in
to revive
a dead man

At times, I wonder
how life would have been
if my dad taught me how to treat a woman?

Would I be in tune with my emotions?

Would I be a better man?

I try my hardest
to be her better half
because if I lose her
I lose myself

3...2..1

clear

Waves of softness rise
from the tips of her toes,
griping unapologetically
as they wrap themselves
around me and squeeze

Her frame, no,
her presence,
is my sanctuary
my peace on
gloomy days
where rain pours
and even nature
feels defeating

The smell of her is love

The feel of her is love

The sight of her is a love
to lose myself in
for a lifetime

Before the Covers Rise like Waves

Each night
before the covers
rise like waves,
I fill myself
with images of you
and cleanse my body
with tears
brought by
the leftover trauma
of being with you

True love is true love
when reciprocated,
but what do I do
when true love
tears me down,
leaving me with nothing
but a broken heart,
torn ego,
and saddened face
to stare at
as a reflection

How do I learn to love again
when all I have left are memories:
handwritten notes,
pictures,
pages upon pages of writing

that utter
the goodness of you

Each night
before the covers
rise like waves,
I fill myself
with images
of the first time we met,
the warm-hearted version of you
that pulled me in,
caressed my back
ever so softly,
and led me to ask:

"Is he the one?"

Words you spoke
flew from your tongue
and landed in my brain
like your kisses on my forehead at:

    2:00 am
    3:00 am
    4:00 am
    5:00 am
    6:00 am

every a.m. until
a.m.'s turned to p.m.'s,
p.m.'s turned to silence,
and silence turned to nothing

How do you feel now that you lost me?

Do you love me now?

Do you finally love me?

Each night
before the covers
rise like waves,
I now fill myself
with images of me

To love again is to learn
how to trust God's protection,
remove myself from situations that do not serve me,
and release all pain
so that the universe
can bring me something greater

Each night
before the covers
rise like waves,
I fill myself
with images of me
finding happiness
with a man far better
than what I pray for

To love again
is to let go
of memories

with you,
to accept trauma
for its reality,
and to see you
for your toxicity

To love again
is to
love myself,
forgive myself,
and put me first

The Greatest Pain

I. My Mother

          At the age of twelve,
          I first heard the sound
          of my mother's cry

Ear pressed against the bathroom door,
I would hear her mumble incoherent words
      as she choked on her sobs
      and prayed for mother nature
          to enter her womb
          and bless her again

        After only two minutes,
     my stomach gripped and turned
        as I wondered if
     she was okay inside the room
         or if I needed
          to be okay
        for the both of us

    I slowly opened the door to find
    her elbows resting on her knees,
       both hands shaking
as they covered her swollen red eyes,
mascara-stained tissue resting in her lap,
    and a short intake of breath
      as she looked at me

and another flood of tears
rushed down her cheeks

It was my brother whose body she grieved,
buried not by
a gunshot wound
or drug raid,
but from medical complications
two days after his birth

It's the medical complications
that no one talks about,
the miscarriage,
the worry when you finally become pregnant,
the pressure to do everything right,
and even when you think
everything is perfect,
death can still steal your joy
in seconds

II. Myself

The brown body
I once knew
expanded itself,
stretching skin
with marks in the shape
of tiger lines
that covered
every inch
of my belly

Times where,
I wished to numb the pain
of your kicks to my abdomen,
the thought of you was my analgesic

III. Baby Girl

The scent of blood
stained on clean white sheets
left a trail to my body in the operating room

As life tried to release
its hold from inside of me
blood came,
blood splattered,
blood swept away my baby
as red blood turned
to black hemorrhage

Doc said:
"Her or the baby?"

Me or the baby?

The baby I prayed for, nurtured, carried,
versus the mother my baby would never know,
the mother who did not raise her child,
or the child who would leave Earth
without experiencing her mother's love
outside the womb?

My Aaliyah, my Baby Girl
will never be lost or forgotten

My baby reached Heaven first
to play with the angels,
paint the sky indigo
and show mommy and daddy
that the greatest pain comes
from within

February 10, 2018

The feeling of loneliness
scares me
only after
the sun's light
sinks down,
back into the atmosphere
and I am left to understand my faults
and fill in stories
with my own imagination

Loneliness is
the thud of metal gates closing,
gates that suffocate me in their lack of love,
gates that separate me,
separate love by double sided glass

With prison there is pain,
there is the chain gang system,
enslavement to thank
for the basis of prison we have today,
ancestors tightened around the neck
then suffocated,
me tightened around the wrist,
then beaten near death
until my voice is nothing
more than a whisper

Society knows that prison
is a melting honeypot of depression,

the location for toxic people
to deal with toxic ways
in toxic environments that perpetrate
more violence
more depression
more misunderstanding
as to how life came to be,
so right for you,
but so wrong for me

I am only a victim of my circumstances,
a victim of my past,
with no solution to mend myself
I am the vase that dropped
and turned into a million pieces,
I am broken

The view of my cell
reminds me of dry coffins
waiting for bodies to enter and rot

The only difference
is my cell walls have a date
etched into them already
because
even though I'm still alive,
I marked the day
I started dying inside

February 10, 2018
the dark night two guards walked in
and decided for me

that I would be
a survivor of sexual assault

The pace of their walk sat slow
as each foot
made contact with concrete
and each stare
made contact with a fear
deeply embedded inside of me
screaming: I don't want to be raped

But, sometimes
we don't have a choice
about what happens to us

The strength of the guards overpowered me
and I watched the entrance of my cell
move further away
as I tried to resist,
squirming,
pushing,
kicking,
crying,
screaming,
attempting to save
the one thing
I thought
I had ownership of:
my body

I sat between two cold walls that night
and wrapped myself in my own arms
to block out the trauma

Little did I know,
that trauma would grow inside of myself
play against my organs like an orchestra,
and force herself into the world
as my daughter

I love you, Imani

Loneliness is fear when I,
a prison mother,
am forced to give away my child
two days past birth

Two days past birth,
I yearn to relive
the last moment
I had with her,
the last moment
I had with my family,
and the last moment
that transformed my life
forever

Would screaming louder have helped?

Would kicking harder have helped,
or would the guards still have abused me?

Loneliness is toxicity

I change my mindset but can't seem to change my circumstances

How can prison ever be good
when it is coupled with separation-
anxiety,
depression,
immediate death of the spirit,
and slow death of the body

How can I escape
my surroundings
when no drug is strong enough
to cure the numbness
that runs through my body
when I am lonely,
desperate for love,
and my prison cell
is the only one
that invites me
to lose myself in?

Virginity

Deacons of my Baptist Church
scream at the sound of sex
muttered from my lips,
but widen their eyes
to my Sunday dress
as it flies up,
tangled within the wind

Pastor dresses in his red robe,
and sits like a King
as he collects tithes from the pew

Preaching at me between breaths,
he screams "Ah" to my ear
and stares into my soul
with intent before yelling:
Don't have sex before marriage!*

I cool myself with two church fans,
one in my left, another in my right,
and slide down slowly in my seat to respond:
Don't tell me to follow a rule that you didn't follow yourself

Sir, do you know
what it means
to hold a mirror to your own eye?
To reach in
and have your own sins
embrace you

like blue wildflowers planted
in open fields in July,
have them remind you
of your past life,
over and over and over
only to be judged
in a house
built on
faith and love

Are you God?

Whether inside church walls or outside,
the blossoming flower
between my legs
is mine,
she is worthy
of love,
of peace,
of surrounding herself
with no judgement
even if that means
removing herself away
from the Pastor
who wrongfully taught her
that her virginity is her self-worth

* Churches who use fear-based tactics to teach about sex are only hurting the children they love. Let's learn to have open and fluid discussions surrounding sex, STIs/STDs, and healthy practices if individuals choose to participate in sexual activity.

YOU

The dark melanin
of your bare skin
seizes me like
Earth's sun
on hot Tuesday mornings

As you stand in front of me,
the beauty from inside of you escapes,
flickering golden light that
mesmerizes me with every beam

The shape of your frame
overstretches my naked canvas
creating a cosmic tie that
leaves my spirit full of you

Can you see Our Love?

Dripping slowly
like raw honey off lips,
sealing one another
as flesh meets flesh,
creating new life

"That's Just *My* Preference"

"Tall, iced chai lattes
 topped with
 whipped, vanilla cream foam
 and a dash of pumpkin spice
 turn me on
 compared to
 the rich blackness
 of strong coffee
 that slides
 down my throat
 and burns,
 no milk,
 no sugar,
 no honey added"

"Of course,
 that's just
 my preference
 regardless of
 whoever
 disagrees"

He says, "Am I wrong for having a preference?"

Of course not.

The issue with '*My* Preference'
is when he speaks down
on black coffee,

sourced directly from bushels
filled by green leaves
and coffee beans

He dogs me out
as he explains his point,
beating me down with words
even when,
I learned to love myself
through affirmation

He spikes sentences of venom from his fangs
because his mother,
a Black woman,
had no time
for his pain,
so he screams:
"All Black women are the same"

No.

Do not compare me
to an emotionally unavailable mother
or label me due to poor experiences
with Black girls *not women*

I wonder how it feels
for him
to run away
from the blackness
that lives within him

Hot black blood bled
creating his Black ass
who disrespects me,
a Black woman,
as if
I asked
for his attention,
his rating,
his opinion,
the audacity
to think
that his opinion
means more
than the self-love
I wrap myself in

His "preference"
should not
put down women
of the race he belongs
or any race at that

I reply, "No, I don't want your sympathy,
your private apologies
with public humiliation
I demand your respect

Of course,
that's just
my preference"

Dear Black People of America

From the color of our skin
to the texture of our hair,
Blackness is a God-gifted legacy,
where every complexion is valued,
loved for its darkness,
and told that it is beautiful
day in and day out

While I cannot face you all,
I can write to you
and plead for you to share this message
with a brother, a sister,
a friend, a cousin,
a stranger you see walking
along the sidewalk
with their head down
needing to hear this message:

You are beautiful

I wrap my love around pens
and write words to you,
hoping to gift a warm feeling
you may have never experienced

You see?

How can I expect you
to give love

when you barely know
how to love yourself fully?

Why do you not see value in your own eye?

Your self-standard of beauty
is now set by silicone shapes
that pump into plump breasts
which force you to hone in
on small details of imperfection,
but those details of imperfection
make you the perfect version
of yourself

How can you distinguish the authenticity of a gold chain,
but fail to notice your best friend
drowning from an inability to express himself
brought by a second wave of depression,
except this time he has no money for meds

He reaches to you for help

He reaches to YOU for help
and you ignore him
because you don't believe in
mental illness, you say
it's a crazy idea
created by White people
until your best friend commits suicide
and you attend his funeral

Now, what do you think?

Mental illness doesn't seem so crazy after all, right?

Wicked thoughts
twist and tumble you
into a new version of yourself
that you never knew existed

Depression creeps over you
as a "new normal,"
a feeling so intense
you know you need help,
but you would rather
"Pray the devil away"
rather than work
with your demons

Why do you not see value in your own eye?

You stand against white walls
looking at yourself
as you caress the point of your elbow

You count four shades of brown
from the crown of your head
to the top of your chest
and panic ...

Where is the bleach cream?
I've gotten so dark, so uneven,
I shouldn't have gone to the beach,
Ugh, I can't find the bleach cream,

I just had it yesterday
Where is it?

... but then you find it

You apply a dab here, a dab there
rub it in, and relax

You hope to tone down the melanin
concentrated in your skin,
this is not sugar in lemonade

How dare you?

The melanin of your skin is irreplaceable,
it is as real as the coil of your hair,
the width of your nose,
and the whiteness of your teeth

Why do you not see value in your own eye?

You walk along the street
with your head held low,
rationalizing if
it's easier to live
or easier to die

"Keep Ya Head Up" by Tupac plays in background

Tupac,
your inspiration, but
you use him

as an excuse
to devalue your brothers and sisters
instead of lifting them up

Who raised you?

A mother,
a father,
two parents,
or one broken
foster care system?

Regardless of who,
they gave the love
they knew best,
A love that still
flowered a soul
as beautiful
and as delicate
as you

Why do you not see your value in your own eye?

But you see value
in every system
that was created
to dismantle you?

You are the chance
for your ancestors to thrive,
to rise from dust
and be born again

Would you die for your children?

Would you take a beating,
or allow a stake
to be driven
though your chest
until streams of deep red blood
run down past your legs?
Death for the idea
of children playing
in fields, running
at all their strength,
unfocused on
the conditions
you endured

If so, then:

Why do you waste time
planted in the weeds
when you are a sunflower?
A sunflower:
vibrant,
radiant,
full of seeds
yet to be sown

Why do you not see value in your own eye,
but you see value in everyone else's?
We are not our own enemy, to destroy.

We must pour love into one another
regardless of
nationality,
sex,
disability,
gender identity,
or sexual identity

We must replace fear and hate
to love each other

Our words, thoughts,
and feelings matter
just as much as we do
even if
the world says
otherwise

Why do you not see value in your own eye?

You, The Black Dove

The softness
of you is felt,
your feathers
lightly graze
the wind's draft,
and you dance
between tranquil breezes
on cool afternoons

Your wings hold the color of snow,
and you fly high amongst thick clouds,
flying in and out of
raindrops that fall
causing Earth's creatures
to pause and admire
the world's natural beauty

Every room in Heaven contains Blackness

The sound of high-pitched, euphonious tunes
brought by Black doves like you
cluster on thin branches,
and sing side-by-side with angels
whose wings stretch to infinity,
your image of blackness
is as natural
as the slow flutter
of white dove wings

Your beauty of blackness
stains panels of bright multicolored glass
with ash,
a blackness so thick
it smears like graphite meeting paper,
A bold blackness,
filling space with scents
of lemon and fresh linen
as you begin to take flight

Your wings expand outward,
as your feet wedge apart,
far enough for comfort,
close enough
for your body heat to melt a single ink-dabbed quill
and fly
without

C
        O
                N
            T
       R
              O
                    L

You, the Black dove contain
the rarity of a diamond,
you are pressured,
then released

Your sweetness
derives from your ancestors
who are concentrated
beyond the golden gates of Heaven
that shine light down over Earth to smile,
ancestors who call for rain
each time a Black body dies
somewhere in the world,
ancestors who pray over you without knowledge,
who concentrate at the entrance of Heaven,
and prepare for other Black bodies
that uphold legacies,
contracts so great with God
that they fly back
over the fiery skies of Africa
to explore their homeland

You, the Black dove release
natural sweet tunes
that yield from
both parts
of your stomach
to capture the silence
of those that surround you

Silence is
the tool to reimagine
the beauty of
Blackness,
the beauty of you
before you fly
away
to freedom

A THOUGHT ...

What would the world be if we had someone like you leading it? The world needs empathetic leaders who are willing and ready to tackle the pressing issues of today. Regardless of which country, income bracket, or religion you were born into, you hold the power to make an impact. The only person stopping you from changing the world is you.

As you reflect on this reading, I hope that you begin to expand your mind outside of its typical routine thinking to ask yourself:

- What can I do today to create a better tomorrow?

- What can I contribute positively to the world?

- How has history impacted the way I view myself and the world at large?

- How can I help push equity at small and large levels?

- What internal biases do I currently hold, and how can I work towards developing a healthier mindset to help create a safer environment for those around me?

- How can I positively impact a community locally and/or globally?

Reflect. Write. Read. Inspire Change.

ACKNOWLEDGEMENTS

Thank you, thank you, thank you to everyone who has supported me throughout my book writing journey. It takes a village to get even the smallest of projects launched, and I am a testament to how it truly takes a great deal of support from family, friends, and acquaintances who believe in your mission. *Black Doves Fly to Freedom* was once a dream, and now it is a reality. I am extremely grateful to you for your time and support!

Thank you to God for His never-ending mercy, and my family who keeps me grounded even in the toughest of times. Thank you to the Spirits of my grandmothers, Elnore "Sadie" Terry and Virginia Dixon Hightower, whose love and guidance helped shape me into the person I am today.

Thank you to those who pre-ordered and donated:

The Stephens Family, Angeline Stephens, Nancy Berkley, Dontrell Stephens, Elsie Stephens-Weatherington, Olivia Grasty, Vivian Tucker, Joseph Terry, Joanna Terry Aguilar, Felescia Terry, James Jennings, Arnytria Smalls, Deihjzia

Fountain, Dionne Regis, Rachel Olson, Gracie Wilson, Gladys Stephens-Barksdale, Amevi Agbogbe, Courtney Acker, Omamus Oghenerhuohwo, Folasayo Obajuluwa, Loryn Duncombe, Khady Diop, Ashley Daisley, Helen Teklu, Paige Yanity, Nathaniel Donkoh-Moore, Francine Lee, Dwanda Lee, Bridget Lee, Tracy Jackson, Geneva Chappell, Denise Jones, Barbara Hightower, Virginia and Michael Sargent, Charlotte Hightower, Elisha Jones, Aldora Martins, Yewande Martins, Audrey Dendy-Hightower, Timi Martins, Eunice Peligro DeFilippo, Geneva Chappell, Javion Featherston, Myrah Lykes, Thomas Barley, Willie Hightower, Alicia Barriga, Michael James, Julia Gilliam, Hannah Goldman, Kyra Scott, Kassie Brown Myers, Debbie Pannell, Emily Lawson, Sara Kirvacsy, Litrele Linder, Morgan Tyler, Caleb Ferrell, Lori Hoyle, Kayla Cabrera, Mary Boyd Crosier, Kelsen Donastien, Jules Tsanang, Zion Harris, N'Derah Cooper, Clarence Lewis, Raeven Mataya, Jordan Corley, Leah Puryear, Kayla Thomas, Janai Malone, Jill Ragland, April Ballard, , Yusuf Onayemi, Godwin Mushiu, Tracy Okafor, Stone Brickhouse, Welby Broaddus, Eric Koester Elizabeth Blair Trent, Terah Ferrell, Carolyn England

www.ingramcontent.com/pod-product-compliance
Lightning Source LLC
LaVergne TN
LVHW011836060526
838200LV00053B/4053